The Heart of
the Orchestra

The Heart of the Orchestra

By JEAN CRAIG

Illustrated by GEORGE OVERLIE

Prepared under the supervision of Robert W. Surplus

Musical Books for Young People

LERNER PUBLICATIONS COMPANY
MINNEAPOLIS, MINNESOTA

ACKNOWLEDGEMENT

The publishers wish to express their appreciation to the Chester E. Groth Music Company, Minneapolis, for supplying many of the actual instruments illustrated in the text.

Library of Congress Catalog Card Number: 62-20802

First Printing 1962
Second Printing 1963
Third Printing 1964
Fourth Printing 1964
Fifth Printing 1966
Sixth Printing 1967
Seventh Printing 1968

CONTENTS

The Strings of the Orchestra

Have you ever heard a symphony orchestra play? If you have, you have surely noticed that the largest part of the orchestra is made up of stringed instruments — violins, violas, cellos, and double basses. You cannot miss the stringed instruments, because there are so many of them — as many as thirty-six violins, twelve violas, fourteen cellos, and eight double basses in a large orchestra.

The first true orchestras were built around stringed instruments. Wind and percussion instruments were added as they were developed, but the orchestra remained mostly stringed instruments. Today, it is still true that while the number of other instruments changes from one piece of music to another, the strings are always used. Sometimes the stringed instruments even play alone without the help of other instruments.

Stringed instruments are important because they can do so many different things. When a string orchestra plays a slow, noble march, the rich sound almost makes us think that a mighty king is about to appear.

A completely different type of sound is made when string players place *mutes* on the bridges of their instruments. A mute is a piece of hard wood or metal that is fitted onto the bridge. The mute stops some of the vibrations of a stringed instrument. It makes the music sound more covered, quiet, and peaceful, like a summer evening.

String players can make a melody sound lively and gay when they play it *pizzicato* (pitz-i-CAH-tō). Music is played pizzicato when the players pluck the strings with the first finger of their right hands, instead of using their bows.

Another special way of playing a stringed instrument is using a *tremolo* (TREH-mō-lō). When a player plays a note tremolo, he moves his bow very quickly back and forth on that note. A note to be played tremolo looks like this: ♪. Sometimes composers have string players play a very soft tremolo for a long time when they want their music to sound mysterious and frightening. Sometimes a tremolo starts softly and slowly builds louder and louder. This can make us very excited, as if we can hardly wait to hear what comes next.

A melody may also be played *spiccato* (spi-CAH-tō). This means that the players bounce the notes off the strings by lifting their bows a little each time the bows change direction. Spiccato bowing can make a melody jump and almost dance, if it is done lightly. It can also make a melody gruff and heavy, if it is done with more strength.

If you have ever watched a string player, you surely have noticed that his left hand seems to shake or rock very quickly back and forth while he is playing. This is called using a *vibrato*

6

(vi-BRAH-tō). When using vibrato on a note, the player rocks his finger so the finger goes slightly above and below the note. This is a picture of a note: —————— . This is a picture of the same note with a vibrato: ⌒⌒⌒⌒ . Vibrato makes string music sound much richer.

Perhaps the most important way of playing is when a string section takes a beautiful melody and makes it live and almost soar. Sometimes we feel as if we are soaring with the melody.

There are many, many other ways of playing a melody on a stringed instrument. Those of you who play a stringed instrument will know about them. Those of you who do not play a stringed instrument may want to find out more about them in the future.

In order to get the richest and fullest sound that is possible, orchestras use five string *sections*. These sections are the *first violin* section, the *second violin* section, the *viola* section, the *cello* section, and the *double bass* section.

These sections are usually seated in one of these two ways.

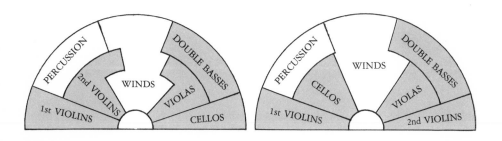

Some conductors may use slightly different seating arrangements. Where the different players sit is up to the conductor of an orchestra.

The first violin section has the melody part in the music more often than any other string section. The music that the first violin section plays also goes higher than that of the other string sections. The second violin section sometimes plays the melody with the first violins. More often, the second violin section plays a *harmony* part—a part that sounds well with the melody.

The viola section usually plays a harmony part. Sometimes, however, the violas are given the melody in a piece of music. Then the melody is played with a "viola sound" which is so different from the sound of the violin. It is a heavier sound, and yet it is a more covered sound.

Often the cellos play a harmony part, but how they love to play the melody when they can! Nothing can sound quite so full and rich as a melody played by the cello section of a fine orchestra.

The double bass section, of course, plays a harmony part. Someone once said that no one ever notices the double basses unless they play wrong notes. This is true, because the double basses play the low notes in an orchestra—the *foundation* notes upon which all the music is built.

How the Stringed Instruments Are Played

The Violin

When you watch the string players in an orchestra, it is easy to think of many questions. How do the players tell which finger to use or which string to play on? How do the bows in each string section always change together and move in the same direction at the same time? Can a string player play chords (more than one note at a time) on his instrument? Let's find out the answers

9

to these questions by talking about each member of the string family in turn.

The violin, like all our stringed instruments, has four strings. Violin strings are tuned to these notes.

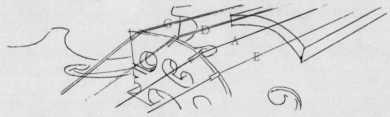

G   D   A   E

The E-string is the one on the player's right as he holds the violin under his chin. The A-string comes next, then the D-string and the G-string.

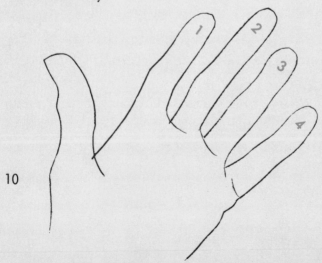

The notes of the strings are called *open* notes. If the player wishes to play notes other than the open notes, he must use the fingers of his left hand. When he uses his fingers, we say he is *stopping* the string or playing *stopped* notes. The fingers are numbered this way.

For those of you who play the piano, the thumb is not counted on the violin, because it is not used to play the different notes.

The fingers are used to fill in the notes between the open strings in this way.

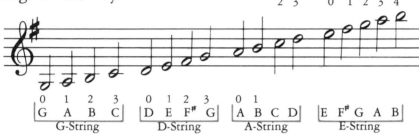

The zeros stand for "open strings", and the other numbers stand for the numbers of the fingers to be used.

Using these finger-numbers, this is how *America* would be played on the violin.

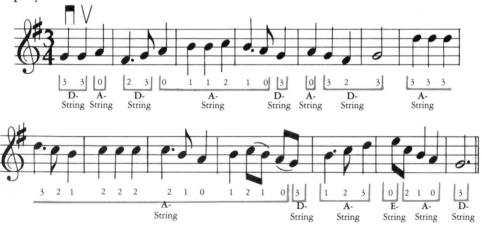

Of course, a violinist knows which string each note is on, and which finger plays each note, so he would not need the finger-numbers or strings marked as they are in the example.

The sign (⊓) above the first note stands for a *down-bow,* while the sign (V) above the second note stands for an *up-bow.* This music is played with the bow changing direction for each note, except for the fourth measure from the end.

The second and third, and the fourth and fifth notes in this meas-ure are connected with curved lines (⌒) called *slurs.* Whenever notes are *slurred* together, they are played on the same direction of the bow. The second and third notes are *both* played on an up-bow. The fourth and fifth notes are *both* played on a down-bow.

In an orchestra, the music for each string section is carefully marked, so that all the players have exactly the same slurs, and the same up-bows and down-bows. This is why all the players' bows change together and move in the same direction at the same time.

A good violinist can play much higher than just the notes we have shown. Our example showed the finger-numbers for the notes in what is called *first position.* By moving his hand up the fingerboard, the violinist can play in higher positions so that he is able to play all these notes.

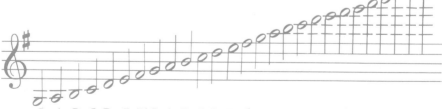

G   A   B   C D   E F#G   A   B   C   D E F#G A B   C D E   F#G A   B C   D E

12

Two, three, or four notes may be played at the same time on a stringed instrument. When two notes are played together, this is called a *double-stop*. The player bows on two strings at once. He may use two open strings, or one stopped string and one open string, or two stopped strings. Here are some easy double-stops on the A and E-strings of the violin.

In each of these double-stops, the upper note is played on the E-string and the lower note is played on the A-string.

Here is a four-note chord that is very easy to play. It is probably the first four-note chord that is learned by young violinists.

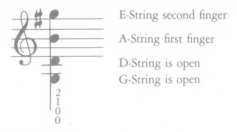

E-String second finger

A-String first finger

D-String is open
G-String is open

This chord is played by first playing the lower two notes, then the upper two—like this.

The Viola

The viola, which looks like a large violin, has its four strings tuned to these notes.

C G   D A

You can see that viola music might be difficult to write down, because such music would always be changing back and forth between the G-clef

and the F-clef.

The C-clef, middle-c

where the third line is middle-c, is used instead. This solves the problem very easily. Using the C-clef, this is how the viola is tuned.

C G D A

On the viola, here is how the notes between the open strings are filled in.

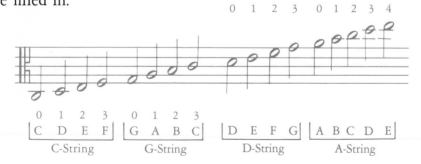

0	1	2	3	0	1	2	3								
C	D	E	F	G	A	B	C	D	E	F	G	A	B	C	D	E

C-String G-String D-String A-String

15

Here is how *America* would be played.

You can see that the bowing marks are the same as for the violin.

By using higher positions, a violist can play all these notes.

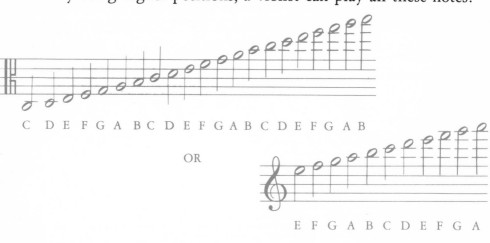

When a viola part goes much above the e on the A-string, the music is usually written on a G-clef.

The Cello

The four strings of the cello (CHELL-ō) are tuned to these notes.

C   G   D   A

Since the cello is so much bigger than either the violin or viola, the notes of the scale are much farther apart. This means that all the fingers are not used on each string.

Here is *America* as it would be played on the cello.

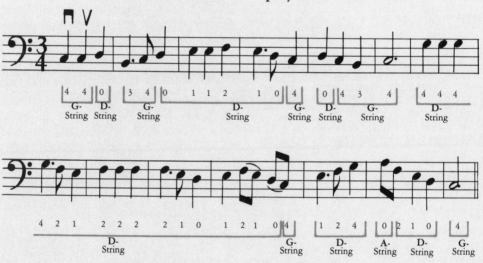

You will notice that the bowing marks are the same as for the violin and the viola. To an audience, there doesn't seem to be an up-bow or a down-bow on a cello, because the bow moves across the cello so that it is always level with the floor. A down-bow on the cello is when the bow moves away from the player, or to the player's right. Up-bow is when the bow moves to the player's left.

By using higher positions, a good cellist can play all these notes.

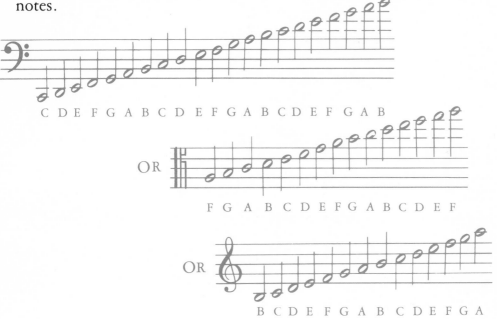

C D E F G A B C D E F G A B C D E F G A B

OR

F G A B C D E F G A B C D E F

OR

B C D E F G A B C D E F G A

A good cellist can read notes on each of these three clefs. The second clef is called a *tenor clef.* Middle-c is on the fourth line from the bottom.

middle-c

When playing the f above middle-c and all higher notes, a cellist usually places his left thumb on the string instead of in back of the neck. This helps hold down the string where it is farther from the fingerboard, and is called *thumb position.*

The Double Bass

The four strings of the double bass are tuned four notes apart instead of five, like the other stringed instruments. This is because of the size of the double bass.

E   A   D   G

Here is how the notes between the open strings are filled in on the double bass.

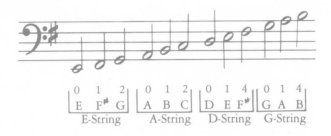

You will notice that only the first, second, and fourth fingers are used. The third finger is never used in playing the double bass, because the notes are so far apart that it is not needed.

The double bass player plays the notes that are written, but the notes that come out are an octave (eight notes) lower. These are the actual notes that we hear.

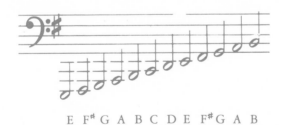

E F♯ G A B C D E F♯ G A B

You can see why double bass music is written higher than it sounds. It is very difficult to write all the little extra lines that are needed to show the actual sound. It is also very confusing to read these extra lines.

Here is how *America* would be played on the double bass.

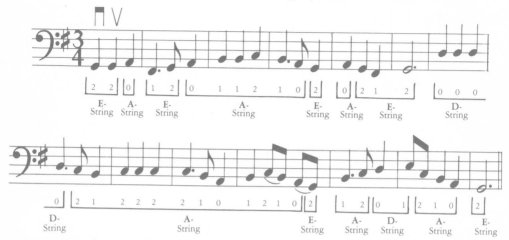

By using higher positions, it is possible to play all these notes on the double bass.

E F# G A B C D E F# G A B C D E F# G A B

Some double basses have a device attached to the E-string at the peg box. When this device is used, it makes it possible for a player to play down to a low c.

E D C

The Parts
of the Stringed Instruments

Each member of the string family has the same parts and is put together in the same way. So when we talk about the parts of the violin, we are also talking about the other members of the string family.

The violin has about seventy parts. All these parts, except the strings and *tail-piece fastening,* are of wood. These parts are glued together—no metal is used. If we take a violin from its case, these are the parts that we see.

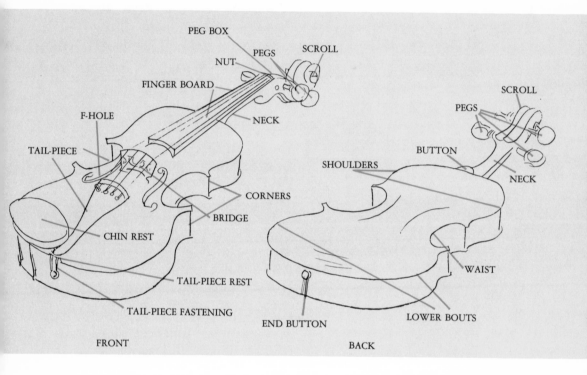

PEG BOX

PEGS   SCROLL

NUT

FINGER BOARD

SCROLL

F-HOLE

NECK

PEGS

TAIL-PIECE

BUTTON

SHOULDERS

NECK

CORNERS

CHIN REST

BRIDGE

WAIST

TAIL-PIECE REST

TAIL-PIECE FASTENING

END BUTTON

LOWER BOUTS

FRONT

BACK

The carved figure at the end of the neck is called a *scroll,* because it looks like a piece of rolled-up parchment or paper, which is also called a scroll. The scroll is the decoration used for the end of all the instruments in the violin family from the family's earliest days. Once in a very long time, you might come across a violin with a human or an animal head in place of the scroll, but this is quite rare.

24

The *pegs, nut, fingerboard, tail-piece, tail-piece rest,* and *end button* are the parts that receive the most handling or the most wear. For this reason, they are made of *ebony.* Ebony is a heavy, very strong, dark wood from Asia and Africa. It is stained black. Ebony feels much cooler to the touch than ordinary wood because of its heaviness. Sometimes the pegs are made of a brown wood called *rosewood.* This is also a very hard wood. It is used because rosewood pegs turn more easily than those made of ebony. Rosewood pegs, however, wear out much sooner than ebony pegs.

The *purfling* is the narrow line running around the edge of the instrument. The purfling protects the edges and keeps them from splintering or splitting. Purfling is made of narrow strips of wood from the plane-tree. Three strips of wood are used. Two of these are stained black. The strip that is not stained is glued between the two other strips like a sandwich. These strips are set into grooves in the wood on the front and back of the instrument. Cheaper instruments sometimes have a black line painted near the edges of the front and back instead of purfling.

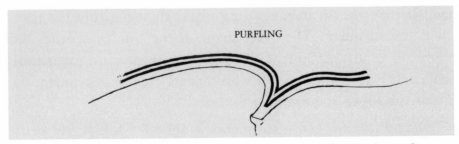

PURFLING

A few makers of instruments have not only used purfling at the edges of the instrument, but also as decoration on the back and sides. Other makers have decorated the backs and sides of instruments with inlaid wood or paint. The designs that have been used are such things as crests, flowers, fancy patterns, and even landscapes! Such decorations might be nice to look at, but they are not good for the tone of an instrument. Paint, inlaid wood, or carving on the back, keeps the instrument from vibrating freely. This means that less sound reaches a listener's ears.

The parts of an instrument that receive pressure from the strings are the *back,* the *neck* and *scroll,* the *ribs* (the sides), and the *bridge.* These parts are made of a harder wood such as maple or sycamore. The strings of a tuned violin have a pull of about sixty-eight pounds on the neck. Not only does the neck have to be of a stronger wood, it also must be carefully glued into place or it will pull loose. Violin strings also put a weight of twenty-six pounds on the bridge. The bow and bowing arm of the violinist add even more weight. Since the bridge is not glued into place, a violinist must make sure that the bridge on his violin is always straight up and down. If it is not absolutely straight, it could collapse with a loud bang, or even snap in two.

The *sound-holes,* or the *f-holes,* are very important to an instrument. If they are cut in the wrong place, they can ruin the tone of a fine instrument. The exact shape of the f-holes depends on the maker of an instrument. People who know stringed instruments very well can often tell who made a certain instrument by the way in which the f-holes are made!

Wood for stringed instruments is aged for five or six years before it is used. This is done so that the wood may be completely dry before it is made into an instrument. If the wood were not aged, it would shrink or change in other ways after the instrument was made.

If the top of a violin were removed, this is what we would see.

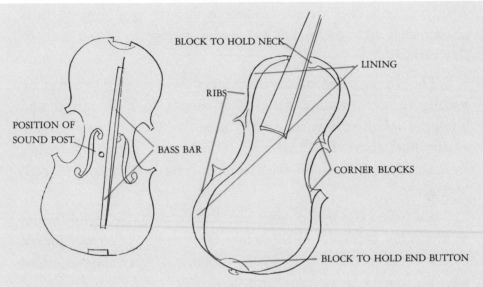

BLOCK TO HOLD NECK

LINING

RIBS

POSITION OF
SOUND POST

BASS BAR

CORNER BLOCKS

BLOCK TO HOLD END BUTTON

The parts of an instrument that receive the least strain are the *top* and the parts that are inside. These parts are made of pine, which is a softer wood. A soft wood is chosen, because it vibrates freely and helps increase the tone of an instrument.

The *blocks* and *linings* all strengthen the instrument. The *sound post* has two uses. It helps to support the top of the instrument. It also carries the sound from the bridge to the inside and back of the instrument. It is set slightly back of the bridge and under the highest sounding string. The *bass bar* is a strip of wood glued under the top of the instrument beneath the lowest sounding string. It helps support the top, and also helps the tone of the lowest string.

After a stringed instrument has been put together, the entire outside, except for the ebony parts and the neck, is varnished. A special, very thin varnish is used. A fine stringed instrument is not finished until the maker has put on twelve to fifteen coats of this varnish!

The *strings* are made of either metal or gut. Metal strings are usually of steel, wound with other metals such as copper and aluminum. Gut strings are usually used by better players because of the finer tone of such strings. Today, gut strings last longer because they are wound with such metals as aluminum, steel, and silver.

Both the cello and double bass have a part that is not found on the other members of the string family. The cello was played at first between the player's knees. There is a story about a cellist who became so fat he could not get his cello between his knees. In desperation he invented the *end-pin.* The end-pin is a long piece of metal attached to the cello at the end button. It allows the cello to rest on the floor. Thinner cellists soon began using end-pins, too, because the end-pin made it easier to hold the cello. It is much easier even for thin cellists to place most of the weight of the cello on the floor.

Today, many double basses also have end-pins. Most end-pins pull out of a hole in the end button to the length that the player wishes. When the instrument is put away, the end-pin is pushed back inside.

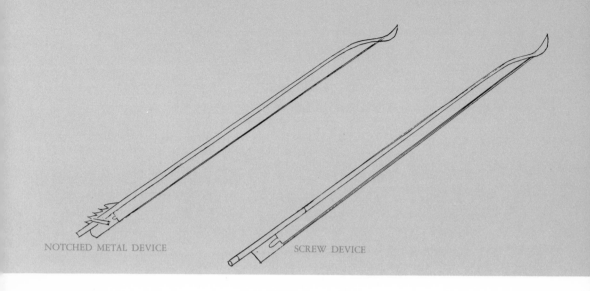

NOTCHED METAL DEVICE   SCREW DEVICE

The Bow

The bow reached its present form much later than stringed instruments. The first bows were nothing but curved sticks of wood, with hair stretched from end to end. The curve in the wood might be very slight, or it might look like a half-circle.

During the sixteenth century, the *frog* was developed. This was a piece of wood at one end of the bow to which the hair was attached. The frog was also used as a handle for playing. In the sixteenth and seventeenth centuries, the frog had a device attached so that the player could control the tightness of the hair. One such device used a strip of notched metal on the top of the bow. The player pulled a band of metal attached to the frog back to the notch he wished. Another device for tightening the hair was a screw which was attached to the frog from the end of the bow. If the screw were turned, the frog was pulled back or forward, which tightened or loosened the hair. This last device is the one which we use on our modern bows.

By the seventeenth century, the bow had lost much of its curve, so that it was only slightly curved outward. Some bows were even almost straight. With such a bow, a player could not play as softly as with a modern bow. Nor was the bow as springy as our bows are today.

The violin family took many years and many different instrument makers to develop it. The bow that we use today was developed almost entirely by one man. His name is Francois Tourte (fran-SWAH TOORT), and he lived in Paris from 1747 to 1835. When Tourte was a young man, the art of playing the violin had developed to the point where performers were looking for bows that were lighter, stronger, and had more bounce or spring to them. Tourte made bows of many different lengths, many different kinds of curves, and many different woods, in order to develop the best possible bow. By about 1780, Tourte had decided upon the form of bow shown below. It is still in use today.

SCREW   WOUND COVERING   TIP

FROG   METAL BAND   HAIR

The main part of the bow, called the *stick,* is made of *pernambuco* wood. This wood is very strong and yet is quite light. It also has the right degree of spring when it is made into a bow. Tourte found that a bow is springier if it curves in toward the hair. After the wood has been cut to the right length, it is bent to the proper curve. The wood is then held in this curve, under pressure and heat, until the curve is "set." This curve lasts for the life of the bow. Some of Tourte's bows are still being used today. They still have the same spring to them as when they were made.

The frog of the bow is usually made of ebony. Some frogs are made of tortoise shell or ivory. The tip is usually of ivory, although sometimes it is made of gold or silver to match the metal used for the *metal band* and *screw.* The metal band is another invention of Tourte's. It keeps the hair flat at the frog, like a ribbon, instead of allowing it to bunch up. The *wound covering* is of a metal thread or of leather, and helps the player to hold the bow more easily.

Today, we use between one-hundred fifty and two-hundred horse hairs in a bow. The hair is the part of the bow that must be replaced as it wears out. Each hair is carefully chosen. It must be perfectly round. Many horse hairs are flat on one side. It must also be the same thickness from one end to the other. Tourte was most careful about the hair on the bows that he sold. His daughter spent a great deal of her time sorting through horse hair, picking the hairs that were good enough to be used on bows.

Once the new type of bow was decided upon for the violin, the bows for the viola, cello, and bass were also changed. The viola bow is a little heavier than the violin bow, in order to match the size and the kind of sound made by the viola. The cello and bass bows are shorter and much heavier, in order to bring out the best possible sound from these instruments.

Today, all string players hold their bows from above the frog, except for some double bass players. This is because there are two kinds of bows for the double bass. The first type is much like the cello bow, and is held like the bows of the rest of the string family. This type is called a *French bow.* The other type is called a *German bow.* The frog of a German double bass bow is much larger than that of a French bow. The German bow is held from below, with the thumb on top.

The Early Stringed Instruments

Where did our stringed instruments come from? Did someone invent them, or did they develop gradually? Before we answer these questions, we must know the answer to this one: What is a stringed instrument?

All that is needed to have a stringed instrument is to stretch one or more strings over some sort of box. This box is called a *sound box,* because it makes the sound of the strings much bigger. The sound box may be one of many shapes. It may be nearly a rectangle, like the sound box of an autoharp; or it may have a curved shape, like the sound box of a guitar. Somewhere on the top of the sound box are one or more holes called *sound-holes.* Sound-holes allow the sound to leave the sound box and be heard. The guitar and autoharp each have one large sound-hole, while a violin has two f-shaped sound-holes.

No one knows who invented the first stringed instrument. All we know is that from the time when man first began writing about himself, he has had stringed instruments.

At first, stringed instruments were played in only one way—they were plucked or played like a guitar. In Arabia and China, about the ninth or tenth century, stringed instruments also began to be played with a bow. The first bows looked like the bows used to shoot arrows—they were curved outward with some sort of hair stretched from end to end. The hair of the bow was rubbed or scraped across the strings of the instrument to make it sound.

Stringed instruments that were played with a bow were brought to Europe from the East. In Europe, such instruments were called by many different names. Most of them, however, were the same in one way—they had pear-shaped sound boxes. Two of these instruments were the *gigue* (jheeg) and the *rebec* (REE-bek). The gigue had one string, while the rebec usually had three.

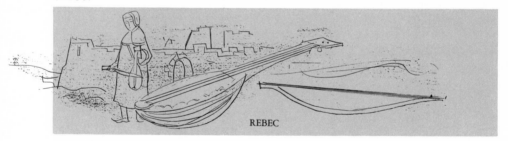

REBEC

During the twelfth and thirteenth centuries, a new stringed instrument called a *vielle* (vee-ELL-uh) was developed. The vielle had five strings. The important thing about the vielle, however, was its shape. The sound box had an *incurved waist*—that is, the middle of the sound box bent inward a little. This probably was done to make it easier for the player to reach each of the five strings with his bow, without accidentally touching another string.

34

VIELLE

The vielle was the father of a very important family of instruments called *viols* (VEE-oles). The viol, in turn, was the father of our modern string family. There were five sizes of viols. The highest was the *treble.* Next came the *alto,* then the *tenor,* then the *bass,* and then the lowest—the *double bass.* They ranged in size from the treble which was twenty-eight inches long, to the double bass which was up to seven feet long. Viols had six strings, although the double bass often had a seventh. The strings were tuned in thirds and fourths. The strings of a treble viol are tuned to these notes.

D   G   C   E A D

The fingerboards of viols had *frets.* Frets are raised lines across the fingerboard which mark the different notes that can be played. At first, frets were pieces of gut tied tightly around the neck of the instrument. Later, frets were strips of gut set into the wood of the fingerboard. The player of a viol would place his finger back of the fret marking the note he wished to play. This caused the string to press against the fret, and shortened the sounding part of the string to the note the player wished.

35

At the end of the neck, the maker of a viol would carve a head. Sometimes it would be a fierce animal head. At other times it would be a human head. A favorite carving was the head of a blindfolded Cupid. This was supposed to illustrate the saying "Love is blind."

The waist, or middle of the viol, was curved inward much more than that of the vielle. Near the waist, on top of the sound box, were two c-shaped sound-holes. Sometimes the holes were wavey or flame-shaped.

All the different sizes of viols were played in the same way. They were rested on or between the knees, even the small treble viol. The player held the bow above his hand, with his thumb on top. Because of the way the bow was held, and because of the way the viol was made, the tone of these instruments was softer and less ringing than our modern stringed instruments.

In England, during the fifteenth and sixteenth centuries, it was the custom to keep a set or *chest of viols*. A chest of viols would be made up of two treble, an alto and a tenor, and two bass viols, which were all matched for their tones. After the evening meal, the family and any guests would spend the evening singing, and playing the viols for entertainment.

The Violin Family

Between 1550 and 1600 there appeared a new instrument which in some ways looked like a viol. In order not to confuse the viol with this new instrument, the viol began to be called the *viola da gamba* (vee-OH-lah dah GAHM-bah), which means "leg-viol" in Italian. It was called the *viola da gamba*, because it was played on or between the knees or legs. The newer instrument was called the *viola da bracchia* (BRAH-chee-ah), which means "arm-viol". It was called the *viola da bracchia*, because it was played from above the arm with the end of the sound box beneath the player's chin. This new instrument was our modern viola! Part of this old name for the viola remains in the German word for viola—*Bratsche* (BRAH-cheh). Can you see how *Bratsche* came from *bracchia?*

Very soon after the viola, a still higher *viola da bracchia* was developed. This new "arm-viol" was the violin. At the same time, tenor and bass members were added to this new family.

The tenor of the new family was the *violoncello* (VEE-oh-lohn-CHELL-ō), called the *cello* for short. Violoncello means "little violone". The violone was the double bass viol. The cello was called a "little violone", because it looked somewhat like a small double bass viol.

The bass member of this new family was never too popular, because it was clumsy to play. Look at a picture of a violin and of a viol. The shoulders of the violin come out quite far from the neck. The shoulders of the viol slope down from the neck. A double bass *violin* would be difficult to play because it would be hard for the player to reach over the wide shoulders to stop the strings. Also, the sound of a double bass *violin* is not as pleasing as that of a double bass *viol.*

The double bass we use in our orchestras today is a viol that has been slightly changed. The old viol has kept only four of its strings. It has lost its frets, and has had its c-shaped sound-holes changed to the newer f-shaped holes.

This new family came to be called the *violin family*. Isn't it strange that the viola was the first member of this family, instead of the violin?

At first, the viol and violin families were both used. The violin family was looked down upon in "proper" musical circles because of its brilliant tone. The violin family at first belonged to the common people. It was used at their feasts and for their dances. In time, the violin family began to replace the viol family. The viol finally passed out of use around the middle of the seventeenth century. Today, viols are played only in special groups which perform music of the fifteenth through seventeenth centuries.

The man who is supposed to have decided upon the shape of the instruments in the violin family was Gaspar da Salo, an Italian from Brescia. The most famous violins have been made in the Italian city of Cremona. Andrea Amati of Cremona, who lived from about 1535 to 1611, was the founder of a family of violin makers. Amati violins and those of the family's famous student, Antonius Stradivarius, who lived from 1644 to 1737, are perhaps the finest instruments ever made. Of course, there were, and still are many other skillful instrument makers in Italy, France, Germany, England, and in our own country.

The stringed instruments of today are almost the same as those old Italian instruments. In fact, most stringed instruments made today are very carefully copied from instruments made many years ago.

The Heart of the Orchestra

It is most difficult for us to realize the important part the fine stringed instruments of Italy played in the growth of the orchestra. These early instruments made the "violin sound" the important sound in the orchestra. The strings have never lost their important position.

There are more strings than all the other instruments in the orchestra. They play the melody more often than the other instruments. No other instrument can do as many things as easily as a stringed instrument.

The strings make an orchestra an orchestra! They are truly *the heart of the orchestra!*

ABOUT THE AUTHOR

Jean Craig is a native of Cleveland, Ohio. Her early musical training took place at the Cleveland Music School Settlement, where she studied violin, piano, and music theory. She is a graduate of the Oberlin Conservatory of Music, with a degree in music education. Miss Craig has taught music in the Cedar Rapids, Iowa, and the Greenwich, Connecticut public schools. She has also played in the Cedar Rapids Symphony Orchestra and teaches violin and flute privately. Her Master of Arts degree was earned at Teachers College, Columbia University, where she is currently enrolled as a doctoral candidate in music and music education.

We specialize in publishing quality books for
young people. For a complete list please write

LERNER PUBLICATIONS COMPANY

241 First Avenue North, Minneapolis, Minnesota 55401